HIGH STREET

HIGH STREET

Written by

J. M. Richards

Illustrated by

Eric Ravilious

LONDON: COUNTRY LIFE LTD.

PRINTED IN ENGLAND AT THE CURWEN PRESS

FIRST PUBLISHED 1938

FOREWORD

This is a book of pictures of different kinds of shops. All the pictures are of real shops, though they are not in fact all in the same street. Most of them are in London, but except for those of a very specialized kind—such as the shop that sells fire-engines and the one that sells diving suits—you could find shops like these in almost any big enough town. One or two, like the saddler and harness maker, you would look for in country towns because their business belongs there.

At one time the shop where you bought things was just the house of the man who made them. The tinker, the tailor and all the other tradesmen sat inside their houses (as they still do in the East) and people who wanted a suit or a saucepan could call in and buy one and could even watch it being made.

But to-day there are very few shops where the things that are offered for sale are actually made by the shop-keeper. Among the shopkeepers in this book the saddler still makes harness in his shop, the country butcher makes his own sausages and the baker his bread; but many more things are made in factories, and the shopkeeper earns his living by selling the factory-made goods to the public. He pays the wholesale dealer, through whom he gets his goods, a little less than he sells them for, and the difference, which is called the trade discount, is what he has to live on—after he has paid the expenses of his shop.

His chief difficulty is having to estimate the demand for things, particularly if he deals in perishable goods. If he is a fishmonger and he buys more fish than he finds he can sell, what is left over is just a loss. And it is not only foodstuffs that are perishable in the sense of having to be sold quickly, because there are fashions in things like hats and jewellery and furniture, and if the shopkeeper buys too many of a kind that goes out of fashion (or that people just do not take to) he finds himself left with a lot of goods he cannot sell. This is called 'dead stock', and the best he can do is to try to make up a little of his loss by having a Sale, when people may buy things they do not like very much because they are cheap. Sometimes, but not often, there is an arrangement whereby he can return what he has not sold and get his money back; for example, stationers buy newspapers and magazines from the publishers on this principle, which is called 'sale or return'.

Nowadays there is such a great variety of goods to buy (and nobody can buy things unless they know exactly what there is for sale) that shops have also to be a source of information. It is only by looking at the shops (and by reading advertisements) that we know what things are available, what new things are being made, and so on.

That is how the idea of the shop window grew. But apart from displaying his goods to attract customers, the shopkeeper has to arrange them conveniently for selling; so when we come to notice the appearance of different kinds of shops we find that each has acquired its own characteristic appearance through custom and the habit of arranging its goods in a particular way. We can distinguish at once between the style of the butcher's shop, for example, with its big window with the door at one side, and with rows of joints hanging up, arranged so that customers inside can point out which one they want, and the chemist's shop and the hardware shop with smaller windows containing shelves to hold a lot of miscellaneous objects, usually with the door in the middle, and the fish-monger's and greengrocer's with their goods displayed on one big shelf in the front of the window, so that people passing can see what is in season. And inside, each kind of shop has its different arrangement of counters and shelves containing rows of bottles or packages or loaves of bread or whatever it may be.

In the same way each trade has its own kind of cart for delivering goods—a baker's cart is quite different from a milkman's; and the men in the shops have their own costumes—you never see a grocer in a butcher's blue apron.

What makes a shop so exciting as a thing to look at is, of course, the quantity of goods. Nothing is more satis-fying than things arranged in order, and nothing could look better (to take examples from this book) than the whole shop window packed tight with cheeses or the shop interior lined with rows of wedding cakes in identical glass cases. You will notice in any number of shops the happy effect of crowds of the same things, arranged in rows on shelves and gay with the colours of their own packages and bottles. They look exciting because of the pattern they make and particularly because they are seen in quantities you would never get at home. And they are all brand new.

Shops have the name of the owner written along the fascia-board above the window. Nowadays this is often very badly done, but lettering lasts so long that there are plenty of shops about with beautiful old lettering, either carved in wood and nailed on the fascia-board or painted or gilded. Sometimes in old shops the stall-board, which is the ledge immediately below the window, is of polished brass and has beautiful lettering engraved on it. The equipment of shops—both old and new—is often very interesting. Look out for polished brass scales, rows of japanned metal tea canisters, and beautifully made boxes and bottles of all kinds. These again are often of special shapes adapted to the needs of the particular trade they serve.

In many places the personal and local character of the shops is disappearing. This is because many shops are now only branches of the big multiple stores, which for convenience are made all the same, and because of the use of ready-made shop fronts and fittings. But it is no use regretting the coming of the multiple store and the standardization of shop fronts, as these are part of our modern way of organizing business and do, on the whole, make better goods available for more people. Even if they do make towns look more alike, and therefore duller, it is a convenience when you are travelling to find branches of a shop you already know. And there is no reason why modern shops need be ugly. When they are, it is often because the sensible customary arrangements that distinguish one kind of shop from another have been lost and their place taken by persuasive advertisements. Also they generally do not fit into the street so well.

The shopkeeper is only one link in a whole chain of events and labours that bring goods to you and me, and in the same way that he has to know all about the goods he sells, people who are interested in shops ought to know the things the shops contain: where they come from and how they are made. That is what this book is mostly about. It tries to answer some of the questions anyone might ask about the shops that are illustrated. Any other questions the shopkeeper or the man behind the counter will probably be glad to answer, if he is not too busy.

J. M. R.

CONTENTS

Foreword, 5

Family Butcher, 10

Coach Builder, 12

Fire Engineer, 16

Letter Maker, 20

Hardware, 24

Naturalist : Furrier : Plumassier, 28

Theatrical Properties, 32

Wedding Cakes, 36

Restaurant and Grill Room, 40

Hams, 44

Saddler and Harness Maker, 48

Fireworks, 52

Baker and Confectioner, 56

Clerical Outfitter, 60

Public-house, 64

Undertaker, 68

Submarine Engineer, 72

Second-hand Furniture and Effects, 76

Model Ships and Railways, 80

Oyster Bar, 84

Pharmaceutical Chemist, 88

Cheesemonger, 92

Amusement Arcade, 96

Knife Grinder, 100

FAMILY BUTCHER

(The picture is opposite the Title-page)

In most small shops the shopkeeper buys his goods ready to be sold to the public, but a butcher, like this one who has his shop in a small country town, has to prepare all his own meat for sale. He gets his carcasses from the farmer or grazier directly the animals have been slaughtered, and some of the things he has to do to them are very difficult and are only learnt after a long apprenticeship.

For instance, veal (which is young beef) is prepared like this: after the head has been cut off the carcass is hung up for half an hour until all the blood has drained away; then a pump with a sharp point is stuck in under the skin of one leg and air is pumped in until the whole skin is as tight as a drum. This makes the fat firm and flaky, which is very important, and afterwards the skin can easily be taken off. A lamb is treated in much the same way, but a pig has to be nearly boiled. It must not be quite boiled or it would start to cook, but it must gradually be heated up in water from cold. This removes the hair. The best age for veal is eight or nine weeks, and for lamb ten or twelve weeks. Mutton is best between four and five years old.

Before it can be sold the carcass must be cut up into joints, like the ones you can see hanging in the window. All the joints have special names according to what part of the animal they come from. A leg is always the hind leg, so each carcass has only two. In the sheep (lamb or mutton) the part above the leg is the loin, divided into two joints, best end and chump end; either side of the back is called the saddle; below is the breast, and in front the neck and the shoulder. The lower part of each leg consists of the shank and the trotters. In the bullock, above the hind leg is the buttock, the aitchbone, the flank and the rump; the side and back are divided into the sirloin, the prime rib, the middle rib and the flank; and in front are the neck, the brisket and the clod, which is the loose flesh hanging down the chest. Besides these joints there are all the insides, like the heart, kidneys, liver and sweetbreads.

The butcher makes his own sausages. The sausage meat, which is made of pork with a little seasoning (such as sage), breadcrumbs and suet, is stuffed into the skin which he makes from a pig's gut. At first it is made in the form of one continuous sausage, several yards long. Then it is pinched into sausages of the right length, and the whole thing is plaited in a complicated way so as to seal the division between each sausage and make a double chain, with pairs of sausages joined at either end.

There are about thirty-two yards of gut in a pig. There is about the same amount in a sheep, but the sheep's gut is chiefly used for making the strings of tennis racquets.

The meat you buy in the butchers' shops in the town often comes from Australia, New Zealand or South America, in special ships containing huge refrigerators. The meat is not frozen, as this is supposed to spoil its quality, but is 'chilled' or kept at a temperature just above freezing point, when it will last for weeks without going bad, as the germs that make it go bad cannot live in the cold.

Butchers wear a costume like the man in the picture: a long, light blue coat and an apron of dark blue and white stripes. He is carrying a chopper with which he becomes very expert at using to cut up the meat into joints.

COACH BUILDER

The two carriages behind the upper windows do not belong to Hoopers at all. They belong to the Marquess of Crewe and the Marquess of Londonderry, and Hoopers, who made them about 1860, keep them there to show what the firm did in its early days. The one on the left is a Brougham and the other is a State Coach, and each is meant to be pulled by two horses. The Marquess who owns the State Coach wanted it brought down so that he could ride in it to the Coronation, but Hoopers could not be sure that the wheels were safe, as it had not been used for so many years. So he rode in an ordinary carriage instead.

Hoopers started making coaches and carriages in 1807, and made nearly all the coaches used on State occasions by the British Royal Family. But when motor-cars began to be used instead of coaches at the beginning of this century, they began making motor-car bodies too, and now they do not make coaches at all, as no one wants them, and the art of building them has been lost. They still repair coaches, and recently they had the job of renovating the Great State Coach which was designed for King George III in 1761 by the famous architect Sir William Chambers, and has been used on State occasions by English kings ever since.

The name 'coach-work' is still used for the bodies of motor-cars, to distinguish them from the mechanical parts, and this is all that Hoopers do themselves. The bodies they make are all 'coach-built'; that is, they are made by covering a separate frame, whereas nowadays most motor-car manufacturers make the whole body in a few large pieces pressed out of sheets of steel, which is easier for mass production. They make special bodies for individual customers,

which are called 'bespoke' bodies (or, in America, 'custom-built bodies'), and put them on the chassis (the framework carrying the wheels and engine), which they get from the car manufacturer. Usually they only make bodies for the grand kinds of car, like Rolls-Royce and Daimler, but sometimes customers ask them to do surprising things, as when an American journalist recently got them to put a special body with old-fashioned wicker coach-work on an ordinary little Austin Seven chassis. They make the bodies of the cars used by the Royal Family, which are all painted chocolate brown with red lines and are the only cars in England that go about without a number plate.

The coats of arms that are fixed to the glass of the windows are those of all the Royalties that have employed Hoopers to make car-bodies for them. They include, besides the British Royal Family, the Kings of Spain, Norway, Portugal and Siam, the Emperor of Japan (who last had one in 1920), the Shah of Persia and the Negus of Abyssinia.

The shop is near the top of St. James's Street, London, and Hoopers have been in it since 1896. It is an older building than that, but Hoopers put in the big glass windows and a huge lift to take the cars and coaches to the upper floor.

FIRE ENGINEER

If you look up 'Fire Prevention' in the *Encyclopædia Britannica* you will find that it says that every person should have 'at least an opportunity of learning how to throw a bucket of water properly, and how to trip up a burning woman and roll her up without fanning the flames'. But for more serious fires special appliances have to be used, such as extinguishers and pumps, and that is what this shop sells.

It also sells big fire-engines and fire-escapes and all their equipment, like the scarlet ones used by the public Fire Brigades, but the things shown in the picture are mostly smaller machines for private people to buy.

On the left, hanging up, is a length of canvas fire-hose. The form in which it is folded allows it to be quickly un-wound without getting tangled. In the middle is a portable fire-pump, like a small fire-engine, with a steam engine with a brass chimney, for using in factories and other buildings. On the shelves on the right, the round white things are metal reels that are used to wind hoses on, and the triangular red things are extinguishers. People keep extinguishers in their houses, particularly in country houses where the Fire Brigade might take a long time to come. Some people also keep one in their motor-car, but these have to be of a special kind to put out petrol fires. All extinguishers work chemically and will put out a fire very quickly unless it is a big one. They are filled with some kind of carbonate and also with a small glass container of sulphuric acid. When there is fire you lift up the extin-guisher and strike the knob at the pointed end hard on the floor. This breaks the container of sulphuric acid, which

16

mixes with the carbonate and produces a foaming mass of carbon dioxide. The carbon dioxide shooting out of the extinguisher covers the flames and puts them out.

The white figure in a glass case at the back of the picture is a complete asbestos suit, which firemen wear if they have to enter a burning building. Asbestos does not burn or conduct heat, so someone wearing an asbestos suit can walk right into a fire without being hurt. The only difficulty is breathing, because of the smoke and because the whole face must be covered up. So the suit has a pipe leading from a tank of oxygen at the back to the front of the mask covering the face.

Other things you can buy are fire bats, which are fire-proofed canvas flaps on the ends of sticks for beating out burning heather and grass, and all kinds of firemen's equipment, like hooks on the end of long poles for tearing down burning buildings before they collapse, and axes and helmets. They have invented a new kind of fireman's helmet, made of cork and enamelled on the outside, that only weighs 22 ounces instead of the 36 ounces that the usual polished brass one weighs, and that is electric-shock proof as it has no metal in it. This helmet will resist an electric current of 11,000 volts from a fallen cable, which would kill a fireman in a brass helmet.

As well as selling machinery to extinguish fires this shop also sells apparatus for escaping from burning buildings. These include ropes and ladders to climb down, and chutes, which are canvas tubes you slide down. Or else you can jump into an outstretched blanket.

LETTER MAKER

The letter maker nowadays takes the place of the old-fashioned sign-writer, who used to go about painting the names on shops and houses and lettering public notices very skilfully with a brush. Several examples of his work can be seen in the pictures in this book. For a long time it has been possible to buy letters ready-made to stick up, like the carved wooden ones of beautiful ornate shape that you see over shops in country towns. These are usually grained like marble or gilded. But recently ready-made letters have become much more commonly used, and particularly illuminated letters for signs and advertisements, which, of course, only came in after the invention of electric light.

It is chiefly all the kinds of illuminated lettering that this shop goes in for, and the shop window is a very gay sight as it is full of specimens of letters lighted up in many different ways. The large P and L at the back of the right-hand window are made out of circular reflectors, so that whenever a bus passes along the street in the evening they light up and look very fine.

The most expensive kind of illuminated sign is the kind that makes changing pictures and sentences which appear and disappear again, like the ones you can see in Piccadilly Circus in London or in Times Square in New York. These are made either of a lot of electric lamps or from neon tubes, which are continuous glass tubes filled with a gas that becomes luminous when the electric current passes through it. It is easier to do lettering by the latter method, as continuous lines of light are better than a series of spots. The lamps or tubes are backed with metal outlines so that the advertisements can still be read in the daytime.

This shop specializes in illuminated signs that are really only reflectors. They consist of rows of small discs of convex silvered glass like mirrors, set in a metal frame, and they are more economical as they use the light from other people's windows, or from the streets or passing traffic, and do not use electric current. It also sells separate letters in wood, glass, bronze, aluminium, steel and enamel, ready to be made up into words, and ready-made number plates and name plates for houses like 'Elmleigh', 'Brocken-hurst', 'Ailsa', and 'Acacia Lodge'. Some public-houses still order gilt lettering engraved on mirrors. You can also buy many kinds of ready-made notices, engraved on bronze, steel or glass, including 'hawkers and canvassers will not be attended to', 'nothing bought at the door', 'please do not ring unless an answer is required', 'please shut the gate' and 'beware of the dog', as well as shorter ones like 'trades-men', 'gentlemen', 'enquiries', 'pull' and 'no admittance'.

HARDWARE

The hardware trade is one that is changing a lot, and certain branches of it are dying out because many of the things that hardware shops sell are being used less, or are being replaced by something else. For instance the heavy stoneware hot-water bottles on the bottom shelf of the window are hardly made any more, as people buy rubber hot-water bottles from the chemist instead; and oil lanterns like the one at the end of the same shelf are not wanted so much now that nearly everyone uses electricity.

But this hardware shop is in a small country town, so the ironmongery side of the business is important, as country people always want tools and garden implements. Also in this part of the country they still buy those blue enamelled tin bottles to take cold tea in when they go out to work (though some people now use cheap thermos flasks instead), and special baskets called 'frail baskets' to take their dinner in to the fields.

Other things the hardware shop sells can be seen in the window: saws of several different shapes, choppers with curved and pointed ends (the curved part is sharp on both sides) which are used for cutting hedges, a sickle for cutting long grass, a gardening spade and fork, a gas fitting, with two small chains to turn the gas on and off, kitchen utensils (a colander, which is a tin bowl with holes in it, and china bowls of different sizes) and the heavy black iron kettles that country people and many cooks still prefer to thin aluminium ones.

This shop window has a Venetian blind which the picture shows closed up at the top. This is the kind made out of a lot of horizontal slats of wood joined together by

broad white tapes with strings that pull it up or down. On top of the window the owner of the shop has put an old-fashioned bicycle to serve as a sign. This kind of bicycle was one of the earliest invented (people rode them about 1870), and was called a 'penny-farthing' because that is what the big and little wheel look like. They were much more difficult to ride than modern bicycles. The saddle on which the rider sat was fixed to the curved metal spring at the top and the pedals were fixed straight on to the hub of the big front wheel. As the rider was sitting almost on the top of the front wheel he could very easily get his weight too far forward, so that the back wheel lifted up and he fell over in front. The tyres were of solid rubber, or even of plain iron, and there was no free wheel, so the rider had to go on working his legs when going downhill. These bicycles were very difficult to get on to, but once on there was a wonderful view from the top.

NATURALIST : FURRIER : PLUMASSIER

When a favourite dog dies, the owners sometimes want to have him stuffed, or his skin made into a rug. They go to a naturalist like Mr. Pollard to have this done. The most famous stuffed dog is the one in a glass case in Paddington Station, which used to walk about the station with a money box round his neck collecting pennies for railwaymen's widows and orphans. He was called 'Tim', and during the years before he died, in 1902, he collected over £800.

The man who stuffs animals is called a taxidermist. There are now only three firms of taxidermists working in London. Most of the work Mr. Pollard does is for hunting people, who ask him to stuff foxes or stags that they have killed. He says he does not get so many wild animals to stuff as he used to. People do not go big-game hunting so much (often they photograph the animals instead of killing them), and houses are not big enough to make room for stuffed animals and heads. But in the past he has stuffed hundreds of wild animals from all parts of the world. He once stuffed a pair of elephants for the Marquess of Bute. He had to mount them on rockers as the Marquess wanted them for his children to play on in the nursery. Sometimes he stuffs animals for museums. The other day he was asked to mount up the bare skeleton of a prize bull-dog that had died. The owner preferred it like that.

Often with big animals it is only the head that is preserved, especially if it has remarkable horns, like the one in the left side of Mr. Pollard's window. The head—or sometimes just the skull—and the horns are mounted on a wooden shield to hang on the wall.

An animal with a beautiful skin, like a tiger or a bear,

28

can be made into a rug. All that Mr. Pollard needs is the skin itself and the skull. He cures the skin, so that the inside is like soft leather, and cleans all the flesh off the skull. Then he mounts the head of the skin on the skull, stuffing it a little where there used to be flesh so that the head is the right shape. He fills in the mouth with 'gilder's composition', modelling a tongue if the mouth is to be shown open and painting the inside of the mouth the right colour, and puts in glass eyes.

When the whole animal is to be stuffed he still only needs the skin and the skull, though sometimes he likes to be given the leg bones as a guide for their length and direction, but he does not incorporate them in the finished animal. A wooden board is used for the backbone and then the rest of the skeleton is built up with wire and wood. The stuffing is wood-pith and modelling clay.

Small animals, birds and fishes are often mounted in glass cases in life-like surroundings that Mr. Pollard makes out of papier-mâché and real grasses and twigs. He also makes inkstands out of horses' hoofs. At home Mr. Pollard's foreman has got two hundred stuffed mice, each in a different attitude.

Mr. Pollard is also a plumassier (it is written above his shop), which means a man who deals with feathers, but nowadays there is very little to do in this line. It was a busy job in the days when women wore big ostrich feathers and other kinds of feathers in their hats and used ostrich-feather fans, and the feathers had to be prepared, dyed and curled, and so on.

The notice in the middle of Mr. Pollard's window is a diploma he won at the People's Palace in 1896 for an exhibit of mounted shells and coral.

THEATRICAL PROPERTIES

All the movable things that are needed on a theatre stage (apart from the scenery and costumes) are called the 'properties'. Big theatrical companies usually have their own property workshop, where they can make whatever they want; otherwise the property manager, who has to see that all the details of the staging of a play are complete, comes to a shop like this. With many things, like bottles or loaves of bread, it would be possible to use real ones on the stage, instead of property ones, which are only imitation; but real things would be more expensive to buy and would probably get broken more easily, or would not last. Also most of the property things you can get in this shop are made of papier-mâché, which is very light, and so they are easier to move about. This is particularly important for travelling theatrical companies, who have to take all their properties with them.

Papier-mâché is paper made into a pulp with water and, while it is soft, spread over a mould of whatever shape is required. The mould can be made of clay or wood, with a light framework of metal if it is a large one. When the paper dries it hardens and the mould is removed, leaving a stiff paper shape which can then be painted the right colours.

Properties made by this method include jugs and bottles, hats, helmets and shields, musical instruments, and the large heads of animals and people like the ones shown at the top of the picture. The musical instruments, of course, do not make the proper noise: someone in the orchestra has to blow a real trumpet whilst the actor pretends to blow his property one, but in case some noise is wanted they are all fitted with a gazoo in the mouthpiece, which makes the

same sound as you can make with a comb and tissue paper. On the bottom shelf of the showcase on the left of the picture you can see imitation joints of meat. You can also get loaves of bread and all kinds of fruit.

Nearly all the things sold in this shop are made in a workshop in the same building. They have to be able to provide any kind of property in a very short time, though the ones there is constant demand for, like policemen's helmets and Hawaiian skirts made out of raffia, they keep always ready. They also have ready the properties needed for the stock pantomime stories, like 'Jack the Giant Killer', 'Cinderella', and 'Puss in Boots', and they provide properties for variety turns, ballets and carnivals. It is chiefly for carnivals that the big heads of birds and animals are used.

The list of properties the shop always keeps ready to sell, mostly made of papier-mâché, includes Britannia shields, helmets and tridents, bald pates, castanets, clown pokers, Dutch sabots, executioners' axes, ears for giants, ears for Pan, giant clubs, giant feet, gipsy coins, horses' tails, jewels, Greek lyres, miners' lamps, noses of waxed linen, orbs, revolvers, scythes for Father Time, skulls and cross-bones, strings of sausages, wooden swords, truncheons and Harlequin wands. There are also many kinds of masks, which are made of waxed gauze and sometimes have hair attached, and false beards, moustaches and eyelashes and materials for make-up.

Other things you can only get at this kind of shop are daggers with a spring in the handle, so that the blade disappears into the handle and looks as though it has really gone into someone's body, and animal skins made for two men to get inside, one to be the front legs and the other the back.

WEDDING CAKES

This is the wedding cake department at Buszards', the famous cake-makers in Oxford Street. They have been there for a hundred years. All that time ago Oxford Street was not nearly such a busy part of London as it is now, but in 1851 there was a great exhibition in Hyde Park, which is at the west end of Oxford Street, and the crowds going to the exhibition used to pass Buszard's shop. That was when it became famous.

In those days the roadway was narrower and the pavement wider, and Buszards had chairs and tables outside their shop on the pavement, as confectioners' shops still do on the Continent.

The most important thing about a wedding cake is its appearance, as it provides the central decoration at the wedding reception, so the cake is covered with different kinds of ornamentation, which is not always meant to be eaten. The eatable part of the cake (which is always the same inside, consisting of rich fruit cake with a thick layer outside of almond paste) is covered with sugar icing, which is ornamented with patterns and with flowers and other designs. This ornamentation, which is also of sugar icing, is all put on by hand. The cook folds a piece of paper so as to form a cone with a small hole at the end, fills it with liquid icing and draws the design on the cake, using the paper cone as a pencil, squeezing a ribbon of icing out through the hole as he goes along.

The solid ornaments that are next put on the cake— things like baskets to hold flowers, figures of all kinds and horseshoes for luck—and the columns that support the upper tiers of a two- or three-tier cake, are made of gum

paste, which is very hard and not meant to be eaten, though it is quite harmless in case someone should eat it by mistake. On top of all these there are usually floral decorations, the flowers being made of wax and the leaves of silver paper, and this is the only part which should certainly not be eaten. The proper flower to have on a wedding cake is orange blossom.

Buszards' cakes are all made in the bakery attached to the shop and are designed by their own chief cook, who will invent a special cake with ornamentation suitable for any occasion: in the case of wedding cakes he is often asked to design the ornamentation to indicate the profession of the bridegroom.

In 1930 he was asked by the Foreign Office to make a special cake for the Duke of Gloucester to take with him when he went to Abyssinia to attend the Emperor's Coronation. This cake was 5 feet 6 inches high, weighed over 200 lbs., and was richly decorated with portraits, coats of arms, flowers and Abyssinian flags, with an equestrian figure on top beneath an oriental canopy of sugar.

After they have been made, rich cakes like these take quite a time to mature and become ready for eating, so Buszards have to keep cakes of all sizes ready in case they are wanted at short notice. They display their cakes round the walls of their shop in beautiful domed glass cases, as you can see in the picture.

All the cakes shown are not for weddings; for instance the pink ones on the top shelf of the glass case in the front are twenty-first birthday cakes: a horseshoe one for luck, a key, which is the symbol for coming of age, and one made in the figure twenty-one.

RESTAURANT AND GRILL ROOM

Although this looks like a scene in a kitchen, it is really one end of the public part of a London restaurant. This type of restaurant is one for which London has been famous for a long time. It specializes in grills (that is, in meat cooked without putting it in a pan, but by laying it on a frame of metal bars right over the fire), and the grilling is done in public so that the customers can choose their piece of meat before it is cooked and say when it is sufficiently done.

The picture is drawn looking through the door of the restaurant and shows two cooks at work, wearing the long white coats fastened high round the neck, the blue-and-white striped trousers and the tall white hats that men cooks (or chefs) always wear. The white hats were invented for the sake of cleanliness. Chefs generally have small feet and wear rather pointed shoes; and they very often seem to have a drooping moustache, like the left-hand one in the picture. He is standing in front of the grill itself. In spite of the economical ways of cooking that are in use nowadays, like gas and electricity, an old-fashioned coal fire is supposed to be still the best for grilling, and this grill consists of a bank of red-hot coals with a sloping iron framework above, which has to be well greased and on which the chef places the steaks, cutlets, sausages and so on as they are ordered. He turns them over when they are half-done with a pair of tongs. He must not use a fork, which would make a hole in the meat and let the juice run out.

The table on the right, where the other chef is standing, is the hot-plate, which is kept permanently warm by hot-water pipes underneath it. Here the ready-cooked hot joints are kept. When they are not being used they are kept

really hot by the silver-plated dish-covers you can see in the picture. These are suspended by chains and pulleys from a metal framework, and balanced by weights (like a sash window), so when the chef wants to carve a slice of roast beef that a customer has ordered he has only to give the cover a push and it rises up in the air ready to be pulled down when he has finished. The customer can come and choose which part of the joint he wants his slice cut from. Inside the cupboard plates are kept hot.

Round the corner on the right is the cold table, and it is also the chefs' job to carve the hams, chickens and cold joints on it as they are wanted. They do this very skilfully with a long, sharp knife with a very narrow, flexible blade.

The part of the restaurant where the customers sit also stretches away on the right. It has elaborate decoration (some of which can be seen in the background of the picture) because grill rooms of this kind were most popular during the last century, when people liked to decorate everything very richly. The woodwork is all heavy mahogany with brass ornaments (like the ornaments along the top of the grill), the floor has patterned tiles, the ceiling is moulded plaster and the walls are divided into panels by raised and painted mouldings, each containing a picture.

The notice on the left is typical of the style of Victorian restaurant ornamentation. The background is a mirror, and the design and lettering are engraved on it with parts of them picked out in gilt.

HAMS

This pile of hams is all ready for Christmas, when people buy hams in great numbers. At this time the provision merchant's shop in the West End of London, where this picture was made, has several hundred, but he has a great many all the year round as it is a favourite English dish.

Hams are the hind legs of pigs, 'cured', as it is called, so that they will keep for a very long time; in fact well-cured hams, like cheeses and wines, improve the longer they are kept, sometimes up to several years.

The curing is a complicated process which varies with the different kinds of ham, but the most important parts of the process consist in rubbing the ham with a mixture of salt and saltpetre, and then, after it has drained, pickling it (usually for about a month) and turning it every day or every other day. The pickle contains salt and usually sugar or treacle (in which case it will be a sweet-cured ham), but some special kinds of ham are cured in other pickles, like the Westmorland hams, which are cured in a mixture of sugar, bay-salt and strong beer, and the Farmer's hams, a very expensive kind made in farms near Oxford, which are cured in malt and are kept for two years before being eaten.

After they have been taken out of the pickle hams are dried, usually by smoking; that is by hanging them up for about a month in a chimney; though the most popular English ham, the York ham, is dry cured: salted and dried without pickling or smoking. Hams still have to be cooked before they can be eaten, and usually they are boiled and eaten cold, but it is important that they should be allowed to cool in the water they are boiled in. They are served at table with a paper frill round their knuckle.

A famous English ham is the Bradenham ham, which comes from Wiltshire. It is the black kind shown in the picture. It is sweet-cured and, when it is to be cooked, after soaking it for two days it should be boiled with a pound of treacle added to the water. Another good English kind is the Suffolk ham, which is also sweet-cured and gets its special flavour from being smoked over a fire of oak chips. Irish hams are smoked over a peat fire.

Of foreign kinds, the most famous are Prague and Westphalia hams, each of which comes from the part of Central Europe it is named after, and a very luxurious kind is the Virginia peach-fed ham. This comes from Virginia, in the United States of America, where the pigs live in the peach orchards and eat the fruit that falls from the trees. This diet gives the hams a special rich pink fat.

You can see in the picture how the hams all have a trademark either stencilled on or burnt into the skin to show where they come from. In the background, beside the two men who sell them (in their white jackets), you can also see a very fine pair of old-fashioned scales made of polished brass. The right-hand pan takes the weights and the left-hand one is broad and flat to take a large ham, which may weigh anything up to twenty pounds.

There is a large black-and-white cat that spends a lot of its time in this window, sleeping among the hams, but when the picture was done it was not there.

SADDLER AND HARNESS MAKER

This shop is in a country town and does most of its business with farmers and other country people. It is an old-fashioned shop, not only because harness and saddles are wanted less since so many people took to using motor-cars and tractors instead of carriage horses and cart horses, but also because of its appearance. The shop window is just like a large ordinary window projecting from the wall of the harness maker's house, like all shop windows once were, before the invention of plate-glass encouraged shopkeepers to compete with each other in displaying their goods in a bigger way; and the window has a figure of a horse over it as a sign of the kind of shop it is, which all shops had when many people could not read.

Although Mr. Smith can make any kind of harness he makes very little, because of the decreasing demand for it and because a good set of harness lasts such a long time— often as long as fifty years. He gets an order to make a new set about once in two months, but he does a lot of repairing. He does not make saddles at all, though he repairs and sells them, as nowadays they are all made by a few firms of saddlers who make nothing else. The different kinds of saddles, for racing, hunting and hacking, vary slightly in shape, but they are all made on a wooden 'tree' or mould which is first fitted to the horse that is going to wear the saddle. The best saddles are of pigskin for the seat and pommel, with the flaps of ordinary hide pricked with little holes to match the pigskin, which would be too thin for the flaps.

The three things hanging below the window are horse collars, which cart horses and farm horses wear round their

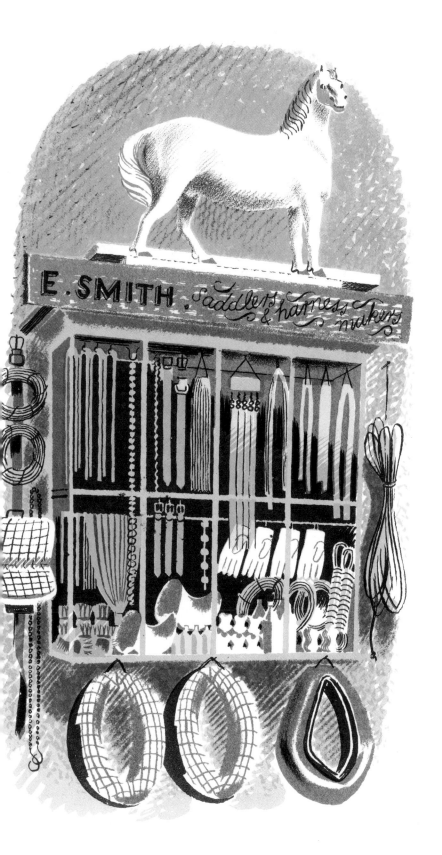

shoulders. They take all the weight when the horses are pulling. The ones on the left show the back or body side, covered with striped serge. The one on the right shows the front, of black leather. They are stuffed with straw. The narrow inner ring, called the forewale, is made first and stuffed very tightly with small plaits of straw doubled up and rammed in with an iron rod. It is then bent to the right shape and the outer collar added. Rye straw is the best for stuffing collars, and wheat straw the next best.

Mr. Smith sells all the other parts of a horse's outfit: stirrups, bits and bridles, headstalls for horses to wear in their stables, horse cloths and body rollers of coloured webbing, with straps and buckles to keep the horse cloths on with, and webbing halters of red, white and blue for horses to wear at sales and fairs. At fairs they also decorate the horses with coloured braid plaited into their manes, which he sells in five different colours. It used to be the fashion to decorate cart horses with brasses—ornamental brass discs hanging from their harness like medals—but that is not done so much now, and Mr. Smith says he only keeps them because ladies like to buy them to hang on beams.

Inside are saddles and more harness hanging from the ceiling, coils of rope and rick cloths. These are large squares of green or white canvas for covering ricks before they are thatched. There are also large straw bonnets for horses to wear in hot weather, with round holes for their ears.

FIREWORKS

This is an ordinary newspaper shop and tobacconist's, but for a few weeks before November 5th every year it fills its window with fireworks. November 5th is Guy Fawkes Day, called after Guido Fawkes, who plotted to blow up the Houses of Parliament with gunpowder on November 5th, 1605, when the King, James I, was inside. The plot was discovered and prevented and the anniversary has been celebrated ever since with fireworks to mark the King's and Parliament's escape from being blown up. Guy Fawkes's plot was organized by the Roman Catholics, who wanted to destroy the Government for trying to suppress the Catholic religion, so November 5th fireworks were originally a demonstration against Roman Catholics, but nowadays that side of it is almost forgotten, and it is just an excuse for letting off fireworks and burning a guy, who is also named after Fawkes.

Shops like this have Firework Clubs to help people save up money to buy fireworks during several weeks before Guy Fawkes Day. They are mostly bought by small boys to let off in the streets, though it is now illegal to let off fireworks in public places, as it might be dangerous.

From the end of the seventeenth century until as recently as 1860 the manufacture of fireworks was entirely illegal, although people used to make them, and there were even official displays. Then the Gunpowder Act of 1860 laid down all sorts of rules about the conditions under which fireworks had to be made and transported, and their manufacture became legal as long as these safeguards were observed. But the chief danger in fireworks manufacture still remained, because at the beginning of the nineteenth

century the use of chlorate of potash had been discovered to make brilliant coloured fires; in fact, modern firework effects date from this discovery. And it happens that a mixture of chlorate of potash and sulphur explodes violently on the slightest knock or friction. As sulphur occurs in nearly all fireworks (gunpowder, which is the usual propelling power, consists of sulphur, saltpetre and charcoal), frequent accidental explosions took place until, in 1894, the mixing of potassium chlorate and sulphur was made illegal. Now fireworks are much safer.

At the back of the shop window are shown the cards you can buy with a lot of small fireworks on them, such as squibs, cannons, crackers, rains and small Catherine wheels. In the front of the window are several Roman candles, which shoot up groups of coloured stars and rains that explode, and on the left is a bouquet of Roman candles that all go off together, after the fuse hanging down in front is lighted. Above is a huge rocket. Rockets can be had in all sizes: they may cost ten shillings each, or even more. The bigger they are the further they will fly, and the more room there is for the 'garniture'. The garniture is what produces the coloured stars and explosions that appear when the rocket has reached the top of its flight, and has to be fitted into the paper case separately from the charge of powder that sends the rocket up.

Fireworks are said to have been invented by the Chinese, who were the first to invent gunpowder, which they only thought of using for the purpose of festivities. In America, fireworks are let off on Independence Day, which is the 4th of July.

BAKER AND CONFECTIONER

Bread very quickly goes stale, so the baker's busiest time is the late afternoon when he is mixing up the bread for the next day. With modern methods of baking there is less night work: at one time bakers worked entirely at night. But still if you go past a baker's shop very late, you nearly always get the smell of hot bread coming up through a grating from the basement below the shop, where the bakery is often situated.

Everyone knows what bread is made from: flour kneaded into dough and leavened with yeast (which is got from a brewery) so that it rises—that is, fills itself with little air-holes—when it is slowly baked in a big oven. Though breadmaking is their chief job, bakers make cakes and buns and pies as well.

Bread is made in loaves of different sizes, and is sold by the pound. The quartern loaf is so called because it weighs about four pounds. Cottage loaves are the ones in two parts, a small head sitting on a big body, like the ones on the shelves at the back of the shop, above the bags of flour. These are made of lumps of dough put straight on the tray that the baker slides into the oven. But some loaves are baked in a tin so that they come out a rectangular shape. The absolutely rectangular ones are called sandwich loaves, as their shape makes them very useful for sandwiches. French loaves are the long cigar-shaped ones, like those in front of the shop window, but in this country bakers do not make them of such great length as they do in France, where people buy them by length instead of by weight.

You will notice that most bakers' shops advertise special

rands of bread, like Hovis and Turog. Usually the baker
actually bakes these kinds of bread himself, from special
flour sent him by the manufacturers, and in special tins
that have the name of the bread embossed on the side, so
that it comes out on the loaf.

At one time quite a lot of people made their own bread,
but now it is only in remote farmhouses in Ireland and in
certain parts of the North of England that it is still done. It
is very economical, as home-made bread keeps much longer
than baker's bread—often as much as a fortnight. The
bread ovens in farmhouses are made of brick and are very
deep. The fire, of faggots of wood, is lighted inside and
kept going until the bricks all round are red hot. Then the
fire is raked out and the dough put in to bake while the
oven slowly cools.

In front of the shop stands a baker's hand-cart which the
baker's man pushes round the streets in the early morning,
delivering the morning's bread. It is a kind of cart that is
only used by bakers. It is usually painted yellow and
chocolate brown with his name on the side in bold decorated letters, though you cannot see this in the picture as
it was done at night. The top of the cart is painted shiny
white.

The baker himself wears white clothes and a white hat
rather like the chef's, only not so tall. The baker's wife
sells bread in the shop.

CLERICAL OUTFITTER

Clergymen, like soldiers, magistrates and milkmen, wear a uniform that shows what work they do, and this shop is where Anglican clergymen buy their outfits. An Anglican clergyman wears his cassock, which is a long black robe tied round the waist with a girdle, at home and sometimes in the street (a thing that Roman Catholic clergymen are not allowed to do in this country). Otherwise, when he is not in church, the only uniform he wears is a collar that fixes at the back instead of at the front, which he wears with an ordinary black or grey suit, and a piece of black silk, called a stock, instead of a tie. When he goes to church to conduct a service he puts on a surplice of white linen over his cassock, like the figure in the middle of the shop window, a scarf or stole round his neck hanging down in front and, if he is going to preach a sermon, a hood as well.

Although the hood is a survival of a medieval garment used to cover the head in bad weather, nowadays it always hangs down the back. It is not only worn by clergymen, but by barristers and schoolmasters as well, and may be worn by anyone who has a degree from a University. But it is useful when clergymen wear one because then you can tell what degree they have got and often what University they got it at. The hood of a Divinity degree is plain black silk for a Bachelor, but for a Doctor of Divinity of Oxford it is scarlet cloth lined with black, and for a Doctor of Divinity of Cambridge it is scarlet cloth lined with pink and violet shot silk with loops of black cord. But the most showy hoods do not always indicate the superior degrees: if a young clergyman was only a Bachelor of Divinity but had gone to Edinburgh or Glasgow University, he could wear

a hood of black silk lined with purple and edged with white rabbit fur, or lined with cherry colour and bordered with scarlet cloth. Anglican clergymen also wear a biretta, a square stiff cap with a tuft on top. It is the only man's hat that may be worn in church, except for the squashy flat velvet hats that vergers wear.

Clergymen of the important kinds wear a special costume every day. When an ordinary parson becomes a Canon of a Cathedral, he wears a rosette in his hat. When he becomes a Dean or Archdeacon, he wears strings on his hat—small pieces of black ribbon on either side, joining the crown to the brim—as well as a rosette, and black breeches and gaiters. A Bishop wears a black silk apron, and when he is in church a purple cassock, a rochet (a surplice with long sleeves and ruffs at the wrists) and a purple biretta. On solemn occasions he wears his cope, and a mitre on his head. Any clergyman who has been appointed Chaplain to the King can wear a cassock of scarlet silk instead of the usual black one.

The people who serve in this shop not only have to know about all these things but they have to be able to guess what every clergyman who comes in thinks about them, as Low Church clergymen disapprove of elaborate vestments and must not be offered the wrong kind of outfit. They must also know about church fittings, as the shop sells these too. Behind the window you can see a row of those brass eagles which form the tops of lecterns, or reading desks. They are usually rather ugly, but the eagle is the symbol for St. John, one of the Evangelists.

A shop like this has one advantage over other shops: it can give any amount of credit as a clergyman can always be traced and so can never get away without paying.

PUBLIC-HOUSE

Like most public-houses, particularly those in towns, this one (which is called 'The Brighton') has three separate rooms to divide up the people who come in for a drink. The door on the right, which is shown open in the picture, leads to the Public Bar, which is the simplest in its furniture and where the beer is usually a little cheaper than it is in the two other bars. The porch on the left, where a man is standing, trying to earn pennies by playing a concertina, has two doors, one leading to the Private Bar, which is a little superior to the Public, and the other leading to the Saloon Bar, which is the grandest of the three.

The three bars are separated by glass screens, engraved with patterns so that people cannot see through, and each has a counter with a central space behind, where the barmaids stand and serve people in all three bars. But if you order beer in the Public Bar you will be given it in a glass, whereas if you are in one of the other bars you will probably get it in a pewter tankard, although sometimes you have to ask for one.

Beer glasses are filled from 'engines'—taps connected with barrels below, with long black handles that the barmaid pulls. Although beer is what public-houses chiefly sell it is never called that: if you want the ordinary beer you ask for 'bitter'. Usually there are also two kinds of ale, mild ale and old ale (which is also called Burton), and you can order a mixture of any two, such as 'old and mild' or 'bitter and Burton'. All these come out of barrels and are said to be 'on draught' to distinguish them from special brands of beer, like Bass and Worthington, that are advertised so much and that come straight from the brewery in

bottles. The barrels are kept in the cellar, which is reached by a hole in the pavement outside the public-house (as well as by a staircase inside). When the barrels are delivered from the brewers they are rolled into the cellar through this hole down a wooden chute.

Most public-houses are 'tied houses', which means that they are owned by one firm of brewers, so that you can only buy beer from that brewery. If it is independent and can sell any kind of beer it is called a 'free house', but there are not many of these. There are breweries in every part of the country, and each brewery controls the public-houses round its own neighbourhood.

There are a lot of complicated laws about public-houses, called the Licensing Laws, which the landlord has to observe very carefully, otherwise the Licensing Justices, who meet every year to administer the Licensing Laws, might refuse to renew his license, and without a license he would not be allowed to sell drinks at all. These laws, among other things, say that he must not refuse to sell anyone a drink, unless he has obviously had too much, that he must not sell drink to children, that he must not allow gambling to go on in the bars, or certain games to be played (especially on Sundays), and that he may only sell drink between certain hours.

Public-houses are chiefly for men, who use them as a club where they can meet their friends. In this way they are different from the Continental café, to which the whole family goes.

UNDERTAKER

An undertaker has to be several kinds of things at the same time: a joiner to make good wooden coffins, an organizer of funeral arrangements, and often (like this one) a monumental mason as well, who provides tombstones and memorial tablets. He is always very solemn, as he has to deal with people whose relatives have just died, and he speaks in a very quiet voice. Mr. Thrave says that his aim is to make a funeral as little like the common idea of a funeral as possible, so he does not make his men wear top-hats. They go bare-headed instead.

Dignity is what he chiefly aims at, and he says that all undertakers now prefer to be called Funeral Directors, as there are so many jokes about undertakers. In America they are called morticians.

Elaborate funerals are no longer popular, except among poor people (particularly in the East End of London), who like to have a lot of show when they die, and join burial clubs to help them save up money for the purpose. In the old-fashioned elaborate funerals they had tall black plumes on the horses' heads, black cloths called 'velvets' covering the horses' backs and reaching almost to the ground, and men called 'mutes' who stood at either side of the door of the room where the body was lying waiting to be buried. The mutes carried wands, and four of these can be seen in the window in the picture.

Besides providing the coffin and the hearse, the undertaker provides black cars or carriages for the relatives to ride in at the funeral, and six attendants or pall-bearers who ride beside the drivers of the cars or else on the hearse. They wear grey striped trousers and black morning coats

68

and carry the coffin on their shoulders, three of them on each side. If there are a great many flowers a special carriage is provided to carry them. It goes in front of the hearse. The whole procession is supposed to travel only at a walking-pace, but if the journey is a very long one—say to another part of the country—this would take too long, so the drivers quicken up between towns.

Coffins are usually of oak (or elm for cheaper ones) and have handles and name-plates of brass or oxydized silver. Mr. Thrave says that what he calls a casket, which is a rectangular box like a chest, is becoming more popular than the usual shaped coffin, which is widest at the shoulders and tapers towards the feet. You can see some of this kind at the back of the window. Whichever is to be used the undertaker must measure the body first, and it is also his job to see that the sexton or grave-digger makes the grave the right size.

In English funerals the coffin-lid is fastened down with screws just before it leaves the house in the funeral procession, but in America this is not done till after the funeral service so that people at the service can walk past and look at the body.

SUBMARINE ENGINEER

The first diving suit (apart from some very primitive ones used in earlier times) was invented in 1819 by Augustus Siebe, the founder of a firm of submarine engineers which still sells diving suits. It consisted of a helmet very like the one shown in the right-hand window of this shop, which the diver put on over his head. It was attached to a water proof jacket under which the diver wore a pair of tight waterproof trousers reaching up to his chest. When he was under water fresh air was pumped into the helmet through a rubber tube, and the used air found its way out between the jacket and the trousers. But the disadvantage was that the diver could not stoop very far, because if he did he might fall over, as the helmet was very heavy, and then the water would come up under his jacket into the helmet and he would be drowned.

So in 1830 Augustus Siebe invented a new diving dress, attached to a completely sealed costume with valves in the helmet to let the air in and out, and the diving suit used nowadays is very much the same. The helmet is made of polished copper with valves and fittings of gunmetal. It usually has three windows for the diver to look through, with metal cross-bars to protect the glass. The tube through which the air is supplied runs from the top of the helmet to a pump worked by a man in a boat, or on land if the diver is working in a harbour. The other important parts of the diver's costume are the weights which he has to wear to keep him at the bottom of the sea. He has two large lead weights, usually of 40 lb. each, hung on his back and front, and lead soles on his boots, which weigh about 15 lb. These also help to keep him upright. When he wants to come up

he closes the valve, so that his whole dress is filled with air and he floats to the surface. He also has a line of rope with which he can signal to the man working the pump by pulling on it, though nowadays the most modern divers have a telephone instead.

Divers in ordinary diving suits like these cannot work at very great depths because the pressure of the water is so great. When they are working on docks and harbours they are usually between 30 ft. and 60 ft. deep, and pearl divers and sponge divers go down as far as 120 ft. or 150 ft. But occasionally in trying to rescue valuable cargoes from sunken ships divers have gone down to nearly 200 ft. Recently inventors have been busy on special metal diving suits that will stand very great depths.

The shop window shows a diver working at the bottom of the sea, and several different kinds of helmet. The window is lined with oyster shells to show that pearl fishing is one of the most important uses of diving apparatus.

SECOND-HAND FURNITURE AND EFFECTS

The picture shows part of the back yard where the owner of this shop stores his collection of junk under a corrugated iron roof.

He buys most of it at country sales, usually at country houses whose owners have died, or are leaving, and arrange to sell the contents of their house. He does not go in for antiques—the valuable pieces of old furniture that are collected by people for their beauty or rarity—as he cannot compete with the real antique dealers who specialize in collectors' pieces and who come down from London or from other big towns to any sale where there is furniture of special value. It is difficult for a small general dealer to compete with the antique dealers because of the 'rings' they establish; that is to say, they agree amongst themselves before the sale who is to buy each important piece of furniture, and avoid bidding against each other. If someone from outside insists on buying one of the pieces they have agreed about they can run the price up and make it very expensive for him.

So the man who owns this junk shop avoids the real antiques and buys the so-called 'second best' instead. His things he sells just for use, but they are often very nice to look at, even if they do not belong to the periods that are fashionable to collect.

The things in sales are often arranged in 'lots'; that is, a number of things are sold as one item, so if you want one of them you have to buy them all. That is how he comes to have things that are no use at all, and that he will not find easy to sell, like the two figures on either side of the picture.

These are plaster statues that once ornamented a mid-Victorian greenhouse. He got them with some garden furniture that he thought he might be able to sell. He only wants 25s. for the two figures. Sometimes he has to buy a lot of oil lamps if he wants a croquet set, or several stuffed sea-gulls in glass cases if he wants a fumed oak bookcase containing a set of the *Encyclopædia Britannica*.

He finds that the easiest things to sell are chairs and tables (the picture shows a lot of these, some of them upside down in the middle), and the most difficult things to sell are large mirrors, which he is always finding in country sales, and mahogany Victorian furniture that takes up a lot of room.

Besides country house sales he goes to sales at shops that are giving up business. Often he can buy very good furniture and fittings from the old-fashioned kind of small shop that has had to shut up because of the competition of multiple stores.

MODEL SHIPS AND RAILWAYS

All the models that this shop sells are scale models: that is, they are exact miniatures of the originals with every part reduced in the same proportion. And they are bought for grown-up people as well as for children to play with. A lot of people are interested, for example, in the way railways work, and have complete miniature railway systems laid out in a spare room or round their back garden, including tunnels and embankments, sidings and goods and passenger stations; also a proper working signalling system.

Bassett-Lowke, which is the name of this shop, sells scale models in eight different sizes, the smallest for running by electricity on the dining-room table, having the gauge of the track—the distance apart of the rails—only $\frac{5}{8}$ in., or about one-ninetieth full size. The usual sizes for indoor systems are $1\frac{1}{4}$ in. gauge and $1\frac{3}{4}$ in. gauge, which are about one forty-fifth and one thirty-second full size. These sizes have clockwork or electric locomotives. The larger sizes, for outdoor railway systems, with real steam locomotives, range from $2\frac{1}{2}$ in. gauge up to 15 in., which is more than a quarter full size. These largest ones are powerful enough to haul train loads of real people. The engines weigh three tons or more, they can travel at 35 miles an hour and can haul a load of 20 tons behind them. Basset-Lowkes only make these to order, but their catalogue of locomotives in stock includes a $7\frac{1}{4}$ in. gauge (one-eighth full size) exact working model of the L.M.S. express locomotive 'Royal Scot', costing £500, and a $9\frac{1}{2}$ in. gauge (one-sixth full size) L.N.E.R. 'Atlantic' type locomotive and tender, costing £450, or £490 with mechanical lubricator and vacuum brakes.

As realism in every detail is what model-railway experts

want, Bassett-Lowkes provide any number of accessories, all to the right size, as well as locomotives, rolling-stock and track. These include signals (with red and green electric lights), signal boxes and mechanism, level-crossing gates, gradient posts, telegraph poles, platelayers' huts, notice boards of all kinds, water-towers, engine sheds and stations. The stations can be completely equipped with everything you could expect to find on a station, such as time-tables, barrows of milk-churns, seats, enamelled advertisements, telephone call-boxes, fire-buckets, bookstalls (including a display of miniature magazine covers), automatic machines and luggage—and, of course, railwaymen and passengers. In the cheaper set of figures to stand on the platform the passengers are ordinary people, but in the more expensive set they consist of George Bernard Shaw, Charlie Chaplin, Lloyd George, Stanley Baldwin, Amy Johnson and Ramsay MacDonald.

Though Bassett-Lowkes are most famous for model rail-ways, they make nearly as much in the way of model ships, and it is the ship part of the shop that is chiefly shown in the picture. The ships are also made exactly to scale to various standard sizes; and can be bought in bits for people to put together themselves. They are either working models, that sail in the proper way or go by steam or clockwork, or 'water-line' models—very small ones that are finished flat at the water line to stand on a table or in a cabinet.

In the picture you can see several racing yachts and, in the middle of the window, with brown sails, a Pilot Lugger. This is a kind of sailing boat used for fishing and other purposes all round the coast, and has a double lug-sail rig instead of the Bermuda rig of the racing yachts, but it is also quite fast and is much better on exposed water.

85

OYSTER BAR

An oyster bar, like White's in the Strand, is a restaurant which sells only one kind of food. You go there before lunch or dinner, have your plate of oysters, and go on somewhere else for the rest of your meal.

Nowadays oysters are regarded as a luxury and classed with champagne and caviare, but at one time they were not nearly so expensive. If you read the books of Surtees or Dickens, or any writers who describe everyday London life in the nineteenth century, you will find oysters referred to as quite an ordinary food. Much earlier than that Dr. Johnson had a cat called Hodge for which he used to buy oysters. Unfortunately Boswell, Dr. Johnson's companion and biographer, disliked cats, and particularly Hodge.

Oysters are eaten raw. Of the three kinds on White's menu, Anglo-Portuguese, Americans and Natives, the Anglo-Portuguese are the cheapest—2s. a dozen. These are ones that have been fished up when young in Portugal and relaid in English waters until they were ready for eating. Even the real English ones, called 'natives' (they cost anything from 3s. 6d. a dozen for little ones up to 7s. 6d. for the best), are nowadays grown in tanks from the time they are quite young, or else in specially made oyster 'beds' in shallow waters along the coast. At one time they were always fished straight from their natural 'beds' in the sea; but they were fished very wastefully and the young ones were not given a chance to settle down. That is why they are now scarcer and much dearer. In America, oysters are still taken in large quantities from their natural 'beds' since there are plenty left, but they have to be careful not to use them all up too wastefully, as people did in England.

English oysters are supposed to have the best flavour. They were very famous among the Romans. Most of the English ones come from the estuary of the Thames and other coasts of the North Sea. They are not found at all in the Baltic Sea, where the water is not salt enough. Oysters need at least three per cent. of salt in the water.

The breeding season is May to September, and at this time it is forbidden to fish for them, though you can sometimes buy foreign ones. You are supposed to remember when not to eat oysters by whether there is an R in the month. Young oysters grow one inch in diameter every year until they reach three inches. After that they grow very slowly. They do not often live to be more than twenty years old. Most adult oysters are seven to ten years old.

In the picture, the waiter who serves the oysters is standing in the door of the restaurant with his tray in his hand and his napkin over his arm. Inside is a bar where customers stand up to eat, with a row of napkins hanging on a rail in front for them to wipe their fingers on. Dozens of plaited straw baskets hang on the wall. These are used by the boy to carry oysters in if anyone orders some from outside.

The oysters are all kept in tubs full of salt water, so that they are alive almost until they are eaten. The man behind the bar opens the shells with a knife, removes the tough part called the 'beard' and puts them on a plate, leaving each oyster on one half of its shell. You flavour them with red pepper and lemon juice and eat small pieces of brown bread and butter at the same time. The right drink to have with them is stout. Experts say you should give them a good feed of oatmeal the night before you are going to eat them.

There is very little chance of finding pearls in the oysters you buy to eat.

PHARMACEUTICAL CHEMIST

It is appropriate that this drawing should have been made at night, because one way in which a chemist's shop differs from ordinary shops is that it usually keeps open late in case people want some medicine in a hurry.

The man who keeps a chemist's shop also differs from other shopkeepers because he has to pass a special examination before he is allowed to do so. Anyone can keep a butcher's or a greengrocer's shop (though to make it pay he must know a lot about the things he sells), but as part of a chemist's job is making up medicines according to a doctor's prescription—called dispensing—and selling all kinds of drugs, it is important for him to know about medicines, or he might make dangerous mistakes. It is also a good thing because poor people who do not want to go to a doctor often ask a chemist's advice when they feel ill.

The chemist's examination makes him an M.P.S., which means a Member of the Pharmaceutical Society of Great Britain, and you will probably find a certificate to say that he is a member hanging up in any chemist's shop.

One of the things there are special laws about is the sale of poisons. Certain drugs are very dangerous if they are wrongly used or taken in larger quantities than is intended, and these the chemist must not sell except with a doctor's prescription. Others he may only sell if the person who buys them writes his name and address in the Poison Book, which the chemist has to keep and which the police consult if someone is found poisoned.

Chemists buy their drugs in large quantities and keep them in rows of bottles in their dispensary, so that they will have all the ingredients ready for making up any

doctor's prescription. Poisonous medicines (such as liniments, which you rub on but must not drink) are put in bottles with red labels saying *POISON*, and of a special shape with corrugated sides which you can recognize at once in the dark. This saves people from being poisoned by being given medicine out of the wrong bottle.

A lot of chemists' shops, particularly the old-fashioned ones, have a row of glass jars full of coloured liquid on the top shelf of their window, like the ones in the picture. These are never for use (the liquid is only coloured water) but are there to show at a glance what kind of shop it is, and are a survival from the days when all shops had signs for people who could not read—like the bicycle over the hardware shop and the horse over the saddler and harness-maker's shop in this book.

Nowadays the chemist sells a lot more than he used to of factory-made medicines and standard brands of pills and tablets that he does not have to make up himself. He also sells soap and toothpaste and photographic films and sun spectacles and rubber hot-water bottles. The multiple store chemists have turned their branches into quite big shops where they also sell stationery and even run a circulating library, but in America they have taken this idea much further, and in the chemists' shops (which are called drug stores) the drug-selling part is right in the background. They sell books and magazines and bottles of milk, and nearly always have the front part of the shop taken up by a soda-fountain—a counter with stools to sit on, where you buy ice creams and all kinds of soft drinks. In the smaller American towns the drug store is often the most convenient place to arrange to meet your friends.

CHEESEMONGER

Except for a row of hams hanging from the ceiling this shop window is filled entirely with cheeses. The different kinds of cheese, most of which you can get here, are usually named after the place where they are made. Cheese is really milk in a form that will keep, and is made from the curd of the milk, solidified by adding rennet (which comes from the inside of a calf's stomach), with the whey (the liquid part remaining) drained away and given to pigs. It is usually afterwards pressed, with weights or in a machine, but not always.

All English cheeses are made from cows' milk. The commonest kinds are Cheddar (named after the place in Somerset) and Cheshire. Both are hard cheeses. The cheap cheese that is imported in large quantities from Canada and New Zealand is often called Cheddar, but it is nothing like the real Somersetshire Cheddar. And generally it has not been kept long enough: a properly matured Cheddar is from six to eleven months old. Cheddar is yellow, and Cheshire pale red. The large drum-shaped cheeses shown in the shop window are of these two kinds. They weigh about seventy pounds, and some are wrapped up in a cloth.

The smaller ones of the same shape are Stilton cheeses, which most people consider the best of the English kinds. Stilton was first made in Melton Mowbray by a Mrs. Paulet. She made cheeses for a cousin of hers who kept the Bell Inn at the village of Stilton, in Huntingdonshire, and sold them there at the end of the eighteenth century. The cheese has a rough grey rind, and inside it is white with blue veins. The veins are formed by a mould which only grows when the cheese is properly ripe. It takes from three to six months

before it is fit to be sold, and several months more before it is mature and ready to eat. The finest Stiltons are those made in the autumn after the cows have been feeding on fresh grass all the summer.

Other semi-hard English cheeses rather like Stilton are Wensleydale (from Yorkshire), the same shape as Stilton only smaller, and Dorset, or 'blue Vinny'—which is made from skimmed milk and is therefore only economical to make when butter is being made too.

The most famous Welsh cheese, Caerphilly, is interesting because of its very flat shape. It used to be made for miners to take down the coal mines, and the flat shape allowed a miner to hold a piece between the finger and thumb of his dirty hands without getting dirt on the cheese itself.

Foreign cheeses mostly come from Italy, France, Switzerland and Holland. Gorgonzola is the commonest Italian cheese. In making it the warm morning's milk is added to the cool milk of the evening before. It grows a green mould in holes specially punched to let the air in. Roquefort, the most famous of the harder French cheeses, is made from ewes' milk. The hard cheese made in Switzerland is called Gruyère. It has holes in it, which are caused by air bubbles formed during the fermentation.

The best soft cheeses (the small flat kind with a thick rind, which are not pressed in the manufacture, such as Camembert, Port Salut and Brie) come from France. They have to be eaten when they are exactly ripe.

The other kind of cheese in the window is Dutch. Dutch cheeses are the round red ones, like croquet balls. They are called Edam. The bright red colour is only on the rind: inside they are a pale orange colour.

AMUSEMENT ARCADE

This is quite a new kind of shop. A few years ago there was no such thing: the nearest was the row of automatic machines on the pier at seaside places, where people with some pennies to spare could amuse themselves playing hockey with miniature figures, or aiming at a target with a revolver, or watching a thrilling rescue by the fire brigade.

The next thing that happened was the introduction of what were called 'pin-table' machines (or Corinthian Bagatelle) into public-houses and cafés. You put a penny in the slot, which released a number of balls, and you tried to shoot them into the holes with the highest numbers. Arrangements of little pegs or pins deflected the ball so that the highest numbers were the most difficult to score. These games became very popular in public-houses, particularly with the landlords as all the pennies put in the machines became a source of profit. The other games people play in public-houses, like darts and shove ha'penny, do not bring in money, though they induce people to stay and spend money on drinks.

It was only after pin-tables had shown themselves so popular in public-houses that a lot of special pin-table shops like this one were opened, and now you find them all over the place—in London there are two or three in nearly every principal street. Often they are only temporarily occupying empty shops, which their proprietors can get for low rents as long as they are willing to move out as soon as the shop is let. For this reason the decorations are usually of a very rough kind that can be quickly put up and taken down again: glass and trellis work, and bright lights and

mirrors. The front of the shop is very open so as to invite people in, and a man stands at the door to change silver into pennies.

The people who run an Amusement Arcade have to be careful not to infringe the Gaming Laws. These are the laws that say you must not play games of chance for money in any public place. So the machines that people put pennies into are labelled 'for amusement only', and if there is any prize given for a good performance on one of the machines it is prominently labelled 'a game of skill'. The prize is generally a packet of cigarettes.

The machine on the left is one they nearly always have. The bottom of the cabinet is full of sweets in which are embedded things like china dolls and cheap alarm clocks. The sweets are meant to be gravel and the other things rocks, and there is a model of a mechanical excavator which works when you put a penny in. You get anything it picks up, but a notice says, 'you pay to see it operate: articles picked up are complimentary'.

The machines inside the arcade are mostly on the pin-table principle, but they get more and more complicated. Sometimes the ball gets shot about the table by springs that it hits on the way, or it runs about on overhead railways and lights electric lamps and does all sorts of things before dropping into a hole; and there is a new kind in which the ball bumps against a spring coiled round a peg, and the number of times it hits a spring before reaching the bottom of the table is recorded by electricity.

Nearly all the new pin-tables come from America. You will see 'made in Chicago' written on most of the machines, with the price of a turn advertised as five cents. A piece of paper has been pasted on the top with 'one penny' on it.

KNIFE GRINDER

This young man pushes his machine about the streets all day, sharpening peoples' knives, scissors and tools. He made the machine himself, mostly out of the parts of old bicycles.

When he has a job to do he rests the two legs of the machine on the ground and climbs up on to a seat at the back, where the picture shows him sitting. From there he can work two treadles with his feet and make the big wheel in the middle go round. This has a belt connecting it with the little grindstone, which revolves very fast. In the picture the young man is sharpening a knife against the grindstone.

J. Lamb, written on the front, is his name, and the word 'chairs' written below means that he can also mend the seats of cane-bottomed or rush-bottomed chairs. He does this sitting on the pavement outside the houses of the people the chairs belong to.

His machine is beautifully ornamented with brass balls round the top and little notches that he has cut along the edges of the wooden frame. He has painted all the notches bright red.

AFTERWORD
Gill Saunders

First published in 1938, in an edition of 2000 copies and priced at seven shillings and sixpence, *High Street* has long been a collector's item. This modest book's desirability was due not only to the antiquarian charms of its subject matter, but also to an accident of history: when the Curwen Press was bombed during the Blitz the lithographic plates for the illustrations were destroyed, which made a post-war reprint impossible. Eric Ravilious (1903–42) himself was killed aged 39 while working as an official war artist and accompanying the RAF in an air-sea rescue mission off the coast Iceland.[1]

The idea for *High Street* seems to have come from Helen Binyon, daughter of writer Laurence Binyon and a student contemporary of Ravilious at the Royal College of Art, with whom he began an adulterous affair in 1934. At Helen's suggestion he had offered 'an Alphabet of Shops'[2] to the Golden Cockerel Press, a publisher that had already accepted a number of his wood-engraved illustrations. Ravilious wrote to Binyon on 9 July 1936:

> The Golden Cockerel wrote this morning to ask if I will do the book of shops so you see what clever ideas you have: and they don't seem in any hurry for it which is as well because I'd have to draw most of them in London before any work could be done. Sandford wants to pay a 20% royalty – no fee – it is to be a speculation on both sides. If you can think of any plan for the book or ideas for it tell me, as it will need some general idea first. You might have a good one some time.[3]

She replied, 'I'm so glad about the Golden Cockerel book – you could do a lovely one & we will go exploring for shops together. Of course I will keep a look-out too by myself – do you remember the Funeral Furnishers you liked with marble clasped hands. I think it should have no text at all – a pure Picture Book but I daresay they will object to that.'[4] The collaboration continued, as did the correspondence, with a letter from Ravilious to Binyon on 11 July 1936 wondering, 'Could you invent do you think an alphabet of shops? A good idea perhaps but twenty six engravings will take time: all the same I'll do it I think – it is a great excitement this book of shops and I am pining to begin.' Two weeks later he was writing 'Couldn't we do this alphabet of shops between us? It would be a nice idea and the idea was yours in the first

Trade card for Toombs & Co.
Engraving. UK, 19th century. V&A: 9457:48

Eric Ravilious, *Trade card for Dunbar Hay*
Wood engraving. UK, 1937. Private Collection.

case. . . . I promise my contributions to be the liveliest I can do because the job interests me to the bone and marrow and so it would you.'[5]

The idea progressed, but Ravilious, who had first thought of doing wood-engraved illustrations (a speciality of the Golden Cockerel Press, and his preferred method for illustration and commercial work up to that point), had since worked at the Curwen Press, which specialized in lithography, and this prompted a change of heart. In her memoir of Ravilious, Binyon recalled that 'after his days of work at the Curwen Press, learning about lithography, Eric had become excited about the idea of doing his illustrations as lithographs.'[6] The discussions with Christopher Sandford, publisher at Golden Cockerel, proved inconclusive and Ravilious offered the project to Country Life Books instead. By this time Ravilious was already working for them on a series of wood-engraved illustrations for *The Country Life Cookery Book*, by Ambrose Heath, published in 1937. Shortly before publication, the working title 'An Alphabet of Shops', which can be seen in an early study for the cover, was abandoned and the more prosaically descriptive 'High Street' was substituted; Ravilious told Helen Binyon, 'It does seem to me to suggest this procession of shops rather.'[7]

The practice of illustrating shops and shopfronts had a well-established history: advertisements, trade cards and bill-heads often included an engraved vignette showing the tradesman's premises,

Afterword

both to tempt the potential customer and to act as a visual *aide-mémoire*. Ravilious had himself designed such a pictorial trade card in 1937, for the business of Dunbar Hay, set up by friends of his, which sold interior decorations and furnishings from a building in Albemarle Street, London. And while they were still students at the RCA, he and Edward Bawden had jointly designed 'The Christmas Book Shop' as the cover to an advertising supplement inserted in the December 1924 issue of *The Studio*; it showed a bow-fronted book shop window in 'ye olde English' style.

Shops also featured as subjects in children's books, notably some fine colour-plate examples published in France in the 1920s and '30s by Père Castor, and also *Boutiques*, by Pierre Mac Orlan, illustrated with lively and amusing colour lithographs by Lucien Boucher. In fact, *High Street* was initially conceived, and indeed promoted, as a children's book. The promotional copy read: 'High Street is a book on shops. All children love the shopping game and this book sets a new game for curious minds, adults as well as children. Eric Ravilious spent a year sketching these shops of London town or country villages. Jim Richards spent another year finding out what happened behind the counter. Together with the printer's help, they have made a work of art.'[8]

Reviewers too commented on the book's likely appeal to children, but also recognized its interest for a wider audience. In the *New Statesman*, G.W. Stonier was enthusiastic and perceptive: 'So gay and vivid are the illustrations that they surprise the reader like the shops themselves when they light up on a foggy morning . . . . The book is

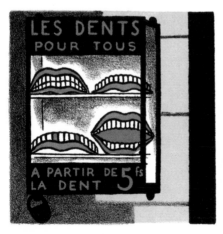

Lucien Boucher, 'Le Dentiste' from *Boutiques*
by Pierre Mac Orlan
Colour lithograph. France, 1925. NAL: G.29.X.44

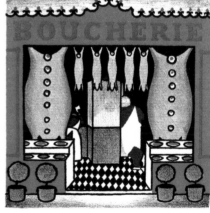

Lucien Boucher, 'La Boucherie' from *Boutiques*
by Pierre Mac Orlan
Colour lithograph. France, 1925. NAL: G.29.X.44

High Street

designed for children, who will love it, but it is more than a picture book. If one wanted a single word for these impressions of Mr Ravilious (on which, it seems, he has spent a year) it would be "hilarious"; there is wit and elegance, as well as gaiety, in every line."[9]

Proofs of three of the prints had been reviewed before publication by John Piper, Ravilious's contemporary and fellow artist, in the magazine *Signature*.[10] Regarding them simply as pictures, rather than as book illustrations, Piper wrote appreciatively of both the medium and the subject matter:

> The delight of his new lithographs of shop fronts is of a kind that is rare enough. It is the delight one gets from work which one feels has been specially suited to an artist's taste and feeling; and there is probably no-one else who could have made these records at once so faithfully and imaginatively. There is about them the suggestion that you are looking in at a series of gay, old-fashioned parties from the matter-of-fact street in the present. They are records of a passing beauty, but they are full of present-day experience. And they are faithful enough to look like tuck-shops full of sherbert, liquorice and lollipops – which, after all, is one of the chief appeals of the attractive shop.[11]

Piper's comments capture the essence of the pictures in *High Street* – vignettes at once realistic but presented with an eye for the theatrical: the shopfront, with ornamental architecture, fancy lettering, and a window or a doorway framing the scene; the use of lighting (the pharmacy seen at night, the amusement arcade lit up within to tempt passers-by) or of silhouette (the butcher's on the front cover, the pub) to dramatize the action or highlight the goods for sale. And the figures, which appear in some of these scenes, resemble dolls or marionettes, heightening this sense of theatricality. Most of these shops, though pictured in the 1930s, are survivors from an earlier age, many with a flavour of Victoriana about their facades and their stock. No single high street, or even small town, would have contained this delightful but eccentric mix of the everyday and the exotic. And though many were staples of high streets everywhere, others, such as the saddler, were to be found only in country towns. Itinerant traders, such as the knife grinder who ends the sequence, would have been an increasingly rare sight in town or country.[12]

Like cabinets of curiosities or museum vitrines, the windows present their wares like exhibits. Plenitude, indulgence and luxury are implicit in the array of produce in the cheesemonger's, the baker's, in the serried ranks of glittering glass domes in the wedding-cake shop, the well-stocked shelves of the book shop, and the plump abundance of hams overflowing the butcher's counter. But in the gaiety and charm of Ravilious's pictures there is also a nostalgic poignancy. The text, by J.M. Richards, which introduced the book and accompanied each of the illustrations, reinforced the impression that this was a history, and indeed an obituary for an endangered species – the independent shopkeeper, and the shopkeeper as a specialist or the maker of the wares he sold. Richards acknowledges – with regret – the loss of individuality inherent in the rise of 'the big multiple stores', 'the use of ready-made shop fronts and fittings' and 'the standardization of shop fronts', with convenience as the trade-off for towns and high streets made duller and more homogenous in 'our modern way of organizing business'.[13]

Though many of the illustrations seem to us extravagant or fanciful, all the shops and other premises illustrated were in fact real places. Tim Mainstone, Adrian Corder-Birch and James Russell have undertaken extensive research to identify the originals of the High Street illustrations[14] and it is thanks to them that we know that of the original 24 only two – the Clerical Outfitter (J. Wippell & Co. Ltd, Tufton Street, London) and the Cheesemonger (Paxton & Whitfield, Jermyn Street, London) are still trading from the same premises as recorded by Ravilious. They found his subjects in various locations; the majority in London – the coach builder, the letter maker, the fire engineer, the furrier, the wedding cake shop, the undertaker, the model ships and railways – but others further afield. Sudbury, in Suffolk, was the home of the bicycle shop, the second-hand furniture shop and fireworks; the hardware store was found in Castle Hedingham, Essex (where Ravilious and his wife had settled in 1934), and nearby Sible Hedingham was the site of the butcher. The pub was The Brighton in Camden Town, London, but the amusement arcade (one of the few new businesses Ravilious included) has not been identified. For each of his subjects he made sketches and notes on the spot. A number of these and his preliminary worked-up drawings survive, some with watercolour wash, others annotated with notes about the colours. As the project progressed, Ravilious included regular bulletins in his letters to Helen Binyon. Writing in November 1935 he gives an account of drawing the scene in the local butcher's shop and notes that 'the meat and rabbits and pigeons are very nice to draw'.[15] In a letter on 8 November 1936, he remarked on his record of the illuminated signs shop, found somewhere in the East End: 'looking very well and I was glad to have got that for the book.

It is a kind of large firework by night, all glowing and sparkling with reflectors like buttons.'[16] In December he reported that 'a few more shops are on the way, and I'm feeling quite excited at the prospect of the book. The diver's shop is almost frightening but the junk shop is the most promising so far.'[17]

The finished book had a wood-engraved title page, but the 24 illustrations were colour lithographs drawn directly onto zinc litho plates with a grained surface. Each illustration was printed in four colours, with a separate plate for each. By allowing the artist to draw directly onto the plate, lithography produces fluid and painterly effects, in marked contrast to the crisp black and white of wood-engraving in which the image has to be incised into a woodblock. Ravilious took full advantage of these qualities, exploiting them to create subtleties of light and shade, volume and texture. Nevertheless, he found lithography to be 'a damned tricky medium'[18] since it required him to work out the colour separations for each image and then draw what was required on each of the four plates. But his diligence and his skill at combining colours (no doubt enhanced by his experience of layering transparent pigments in watercolour painting) resulted in richly coloured illustrations that belie the limitations of the process. Certainly this was an achievement remarked upon by reviewers, with Raymond Mortimer declaring, 'His lithographs are very subtly and

Kenneth Rowntree, *House at Easingwold, Yorkshire*
Watercolour. UK, 1940. V&A: E.2576–1949

Afterword

delightfully coloured . . . lovely to look at and lively to read . . . this book is an object lesson in the pleasure of using one's eyes'.[19]

High Street — though an idiosyncratic and in many ways personal project — was very much of its period. There was a growing enthusiasm for vernacular architecture, and a revival of interest in Victorian popular arts was manifest in critical writing, as well as in art and design, in reaction to the overriding influence of the streamlined functionality of Modernism, which eschewed ornament and nostalgia. There is, too, more than a hint of the Surrealists' influence in the way in which Ravilious presented many of these everyday emporia as strange and marvellous, investing the prosaic with an air of novelty, juxtaposing the familiar and the fantastic, order with excess. Underneath the playfulness and charm remarked on by the critics, there was also something unsettling and mysterious. Ravilious was not alone in appreciating the appeal of shops as subjects for pictures. Several of his contemporaries saw shops and shopfronts as evocative emblems of local identity, and admired them as manifestations of English popular art. Working for the Recording Britain scheme in the early 1940s, several contributors — among them Barbara Jones, Enid Marx and Kenneth Rowntree — indulged their enthusiasm for such things as inn- and shop-signs, high-street shops, and public houses. After the war, Jones published *The Unsophisticated Arts*, an account of popular arts and crafts, which included examples of shopfront decoration such as Bateman's Optician's in Croydon, embellished with signs showing giant eyes and spectacles.[20] In a later book she wrote approvingly of shops as subjects for pictures, setting out their aesthetic attractions: 'Small shops often present most elegant arrangements of fascia, windows, and doors, and sometimes of merchandize (gunsmiths, ironmongers, greengrocers, fishmongers, etc.), and sometimes of lettering.'[21] Readers of *High Street* would be inclined to agree.

An optician's shop in George Street, Croydon.

155

Barbara Jones, 'Bateman's Optician' from *The Unsophisticated Arts*
United Kingdom, 1951. NAL: 219.K.8

1 In writing this introduction to *High Street* I have been indebted to the exhaustive research by Tim Mainstone, Alan Powers and James Russell, published in *Eric Ravilious: The Story of High Street*, The Mainstone Press, 2008.

2 Helen Binyon to Pat Gilmour, 26 November 1976, Tate Gallery Records TG92/316/17 Ravilious (quoted in Powers and Russell, op.cit., p.111).

3 Eric Ravilious to Helen Binyon, 9 July 1935, East Sussex Record Office (quoted in Powers and Russell, op.cit., p.112).

4 Quoted in Powers and Russell, op.cit., p.112.

5 Quoted in Powers and Russell, op.cit., p.112.

6 Helen Binyon, Eric Ravilious, *Memoir of an Artist*, Guildford and London, Lutterworth Press, 1983, p.82 (quoted in Powers and Russell, op.cit., p.118).

7 Quoted in Powers and Russell, op.cit., p.170.

8 Quoted in Powers and Russell, op.cit., p.190.

9 G.W. Stonier, 'Cigarette Cards of London', *New Statesman*, vol.16, 19 November 1938, p.834 (quoted in Powers and Russell, op.cit., p.192).

10 These were Restaurant and Grill Room; Letter Maker; and Naturalist: Furrier: Plumassier. All were substantially reworked for publication in *High Street*, with adjustments to colour and the addition of various details.

11 *Signature*, no.5, March 1937, p.48

12 Enid Marx, in her watercolour *Chemist's Shop, Circus Road, St John's Wood, c.*1940 [V&A: E.1840–1949], painted for the Recording Britain scheme, also shows a knife grinder, as one of the 'changing' or 'vanishing' aspects of British life and landscape.

13 *High Street*, foreword, p.8.

14 See Powers and Russell, op.cit., pp.223–279.

15 ER to HB, 6 November 1935, ESRO (quoted in Powers and Russell, op.cit., p.147).

16 ER to HB, 8 November 1936, ESRO (quoted in Powers and Russell, op.cit., p.150).

17 ER to HB, 6 December, 1936, ESRO (quoted in Powers and Russell, op.cit., p.150).

18 Letter to Diana Tuely, 1 April, 1941, quoted in Gaye Smith, *Eric Ravilious in Print: Books, Wood, Engraving, Lithography and Ceramics*, Manchester Metropolitan University, 2003, exh. cat., p.11.

19 Raymond Mortimer, *Architectural Review*, January 1939, p.44.

20 Jones, *The Unsophisticated Arts*, Architectural Press, 1951, p.155.

21 Barbara Jones, *Water-Colour Painting*, A & C Black, 1960, p.ix.

Afterword

Original English language edition first published in 1938 by Country Life Publications. This edition reproduced by permission of Egmont UK Limited, 239 Kensington High Street, London W8 6SA. All rights reserved.

This edition first published by V&A Publishing, 2012

Victoria and Albert Museum
South Kensington
London SW7 2RL

www.vandabooks.com

Distributed in North America by Harry N. Abrams Inc., New York

Afterword by Gill Saunders © The Board of Trustees of the Victoria and Albert Museum, 2012

The moral right of the author has been asserted.

ISBN 978 1 85177 689 4

Library of Congress Control Number 2011935129

10 9 8 7 6 5 4 3 2 1
2016 2015 2014 2013 2012

A catalogue record for this book is available from the British Library.

Pages 102–3: Eric Ravilious, design for an end paper. Colour offset lithograph, 1920s or '30s. V&A: E.1678–1929

The images by Eric Ravilious on pages 102–3 and 105 are © Estate of Eric Ravilious. All rights reserved, DACS 2012

Printed in China by C&C Offset Printing Co. Ltd.

V&A Publishing

Supporting the world's leading museum of art and design, the Victoria and Albert Museum, London